T0137561

Joseph T. Reese

Street Stories

God's Glory

Spread the Good News

Order this book online at www.trafford.com
or email orders@trafford.com

Most Trafford titles are also available at major online book retailers.

Printed in the United States of America.

ISBN: 978-1-4269-5107-7 (sc)
ISBN: 978-1-4269-5108-4 (e)

Trafford rev. 12/06/2011

 www.trafford.com

North America & international
toll-free: 1 888 232 4444 (USA & Canada)
phone: 250 383 6864 ◆ fax: 812 355 4082

Dedication

I give the highest praise "Al le luia" to Jehovah God, thanking Him for pouring out his Holy Spirit on me.

I want to thank my grandparents, parents, family, friends, neighbors, turtlecreek, fans global and haters.

Acknowledgements

I thank God for makin' my name famous: Joseph T. Reese from Indianapolis, Indiana. I'm all about my Father's business. I'm here to Spread the Good News to all mankind of all generations in the world. This is real talk. Thus, these prophetic words indicate that there would come one who had the legal right to receive "The Scepter" or sovereignty, and "the Commander's Staff" or rulership over "the Peoples" of all mankind. Who would this One Be?

Foreword

It is a very responsible thing to translate these Street Stories/God's Glory; I was inspired by God to write down for our benefit today. Enjoy these wonderful stories and allow the power of the Holy Spirit to speak to you, convict you and improve your daily living. God will be Glorified!

Street Stories

God's Glory

Street Stories
The First Half

Makin' Power Moves

I ended `05 as a soldier. I started `06 as a warrior. I thank God for that change. He said I'll be perfect for that part. From the 1st to the 4th generation, the well ran low. Now the 3rd and 4th generations are makin' power moves to overflow the well – maintain the flow for the plus generations that's on the right path. For the loved ones that fell off the family tree one day, we will see each other again to live rich in Heaven. I hope the good outweighs the bad things they did. From the 1st generation we were taught the Word, and to teach it to all generations so we can all live again. Enemies might survive the 1st round, but at the end of the battle, my partner and I will stand up with our hands in the air for victory over our enemies. Enemies want to put my Light out. It might happen one day, so live right by the Law and have fun, because you will live forever in Heaven, where the Light will never go out.

This Is Deep!

This is deep, "B.J." let them know!
Yep! That's what I'm here for!

What's up all nations! The Lord has saved us!

The Lord is the greatest God. King over all other gods.
He holds the deepest part of the Earth in His hands.
The mountain peaks belong to Him. The ocean is the
Lord's because He made it. With His own hands He
formed the dry land. Bow down and worship the Lord
our Creator!

Psalm 95:3-6

This is deep! Got my fans feelin' it in their heads to their feet. At house parties and clubs, shakin' it up to the *Street Stories* that we got in your hometown. On a money-makin' mission, now I got things that make evil minds click to take my 2nd half that I worked hard for at home and studio. The same thing clicked in my mind, but I never did it 'cause I knew my day would come. You know how the story goes, from listenin' to those S.S.P. (street story productions) hits from the Midwest. No more ups and downs like the weather. My savings account keeps goin' like eternity. My life is in danger for the things I have. Hittin' different hometowns to find high-class women to get my game on so the party can start and they can tell all their high-class friends about Big Jiggy — that's a high-class man. That's what I call females and males who live Ist class. Just some hood girls and boys that made it in life. Hood girls and high-class women ask me, "Why they call you Big Jiggy?" 'Cause I'm big! Do you want to see or feel, just to make them lust? Gettin' fresh again, changing cars, rollin' with them Warriors from Indy, lookin' for all y'all Big Chrome Rims lovers. Boys want to ride on your team; ain't makin' net pay, want you to buy them something every day. I let them boys know quick, they can't ride, and a shakedown for the girls. If you want to ride with some Warriors that don't give a care, 'cause we are all legit with our D.R.I. (drivers' license, registration, and insurance)... just in case we get pulled over by the blue nights. They let us go after seein' it. We roll out holdin' tres out the window. Some of the girls turned into fiends that I went to school with. Didn't give me no play. Now, when they see me, they ask me for some money.

Read Between the Lines for the World

"I will use stories to speak my message and to explain things that have been since the creation of the world."

Matthew 13:35

The world is wicked. We need to save it for the One that made it. Look back at the ones who have faith to come up in the race. The man made the world wicked. Like some bad weeds in a garden field, they need to be pulled out of the ground, thrown into a plow to be burned. Then the ground will be fresh and clean the way God wanted it. Pray morning, noon, and night that we will win the battle over our enemies. Start in your homes, then spread the love to make the earth peaceful like Heaven. Black Gods, Kings and Queens were to worship the Messiah in the new world. Whence forth this planet is ours by divine birthright. One man took advantage of another man's capacity to love. One man perverted and turned these principles against the other man. This beast then cheated and tricked Africa into the most horrible form of bondage and slavery ever known to mankind. Our knowledge has been locked up in the dungeon for over 400 years. The original man was created as an upright, beautiful, Black being in the image of God on earth. Therefore, we must act like it and teach our children the Word so that they can stop regressing. I'm working hard to get my message out to the world.

I WAS SENT TO DO THIS WORK

How Many Generations Does It Take To Get It Together?

From the 1st to the 4th generation, the well ran low. Now the 3rd and 4th generation is makin' power moves to overflow the well. Maintain the flow for the plus generation on the right path. Teach them the Word and the working fields we will leave behind. For the loved ones that fell off the family tree. One day, we will see each other again to live rich in Heaven while our children live rich on earth. They will miss us, but they will know right from wrong. God will open up Heaven's pearly gates for them. From the 1st generation, we were taught the Word and to teach it to all generations so we all can live again. Enemies, don't be surprised when you die and the Light doesn't turn on. You won't live again for your sins on earth. In to a snake hole you will go with the rest of the evil ones on the devil's side (no good for the Almighty God side). Enemies might defeat us on earth, but we will live again, and we will have the last laugh, but they will have the last cry. From the 4th plus generation, we will have bigger and better things. Our people are powerless, oppressed, and in some cases, outright corrupt. Therefore, we need all the love, understanding, and patience that we can get from each other. It is our sincere prayer that God will give Black people the understanding to see the importance of this philosophy, for it deals directly with our survival as people. The world is indebted to us for our contributions in culture, art, science, religion, government, and other cornerstones of civilization. Now the time has come when we must use Love to gain power so that we will no longer be sniveling, pitiful doormats for others to wipe their feet on. Put out of your mind the idea that we must always prove to someone that we don't dislike them because of oppression or for making the world wicked.

VICTORY OVER MY ENEMIES

(Why They Want to Kill Me?)

I have a Boston (13) in my hand, shoutin' "Next" after spending it. Enemies are in line wantin' a winnin' hand, but my partner and I have each other's back. Enemies might survive the 1st round, but at the end of the battle, my partner and I will stand up with our hands in the air because we will be victorious over all of our enemies. Love and obey God's commandments and His people. The Good News is being spread nationwide. My words and my kindness are being disobeyed by many enemies that want to put out my light. One day it might happen. Live right by the laws and have fun, 'cause you will live forever in heaven, where the Light will never go out. I'm shining bright like the sun on earth. It's hard to get near me without burnin' up. Some say I'm crazy, but I'm just havin' fun. I never leave home without packin' my Sword. Jumping in my whip (car) by a push of a button, I'm ready to go, top down on my candy 6 – 4. Hit a switch, I'm off the flo' creepin' out real slow. Dressed up so fly like I'm in a fashion show, tryin' not to step on any toes ('cause I know it can hurt). Enemies got to overlook the healthy ones, 'cause one day it might come to them.

Don't Let Them Stop Your Shine Get Your License and Your Pink Sheet

Money! O yeah! Second half feels great. Pockets are full with big heads. Wallet is full with plastic cards. Having faith is going to make it last a long time. Knocking haters out of the race for trying to take my place. Putting tears on their family faces, keeping my roll on, looking back at the ones who have faith to come up in the race to see what I can do to help them. Fly straight, and you will go right to the top and shine with the rest of the stars. Get your license and your pink sheet, 'cause the laws and the haters will stop you from rolling too hard. Call your lawyer for the laws harassing you. Call 9-1-1 for the haters that foul out in the paint. Roll with someone to be an eyewitness. Those bloody fools didn't know who they were messing with. Now they know to show me respect. Goin' home to change whips. Some say I'm crazy, but I'm just havin' fun. When they see my plates (and it reads RESPECT ME), they just pass me by rollin' side to side just doin' it. Parking my whip enough clowning for today. It's time to check on my money that I made for today. It's a whole new day. Time to pack up and tour from place to place to see how other hometowns react on Street Stories/God's Glory. They are lovin' it! Droppin' it like it's hot! Rolling off, banging it. Joe Reese gets a call back. Let's make a deal, the price is right. Now we have more shows to do. Pullin' all-nighters, makin' all that money to continue our shine. Between shows, we judge with ladies who are coming along to keep us company. Shooting videos to make a higher rank so that we end up in first place.

Hold Down Bro.

Hold down Bro, Indianapolis is on the scene. We got a pocket full of green. Get those girls off of their knees and pray for our enemies.

Now we receive our Master's breakthrough, it's time to roll out and show these sleepers what Indy's all about. Blow your brains out with the Word, not the herb. Ain't nothing changed. We still roll back to back in our updated toys, while last years' is at home for our girls and boys.
Flossin' so hard, makin our enemies stress even harder, livin' in the last days, so we got to make a change. When Jesus returns, the wicked ones will burn.
Get those girls off of their knees. I have a job for them. Fill out this application if you don't like being called "B's". Your knees are dusty and rusty from being down too long. Now you are on my team. You can move on to bigger and better things. So spread the Good News to your fam and friends. I was sent to do this work, so we can all have things.
Well, that's how it blows. When you don't get chosen. Don't give up! We fall down, but we can get up! What you are going through, I've been through. That's the

wrong path. Change like me and enjoy your second half. We can hustle in these fields and stay clean. Everyone will love and respect us. You know what I mean.

Yes, we stay fresh from head to toe.

Watch out for your enemies that want to step on our toes.

STOP TELLIN' BAD STORIES AND TEACH THE TRUTH

COMIN' THROUGH THE PLACE WITH
THAT MESS. LET THE PEACE REST
COMPLETELY. YOU ALL ARE LIKE ROTTIN'
APPLES, SPOILING THE BUNCH. IT'S TIME
TO MAKE A CHANGE IN Y'ALL STORY-
TELLIN'. THE WORLD IS BRAINWASHED
FROM THAT MESS. THE PEACE CAN'T GAIN
IF Y'ALL DON'T MAKE THAT CHANGE.
Y'ALL FANS WILL LOVE Y'ALL THE SAME,
AND Y'ALL WILL GAIN NEW FANS BY
TELLIN' GOOD STORIES. LET'S TRY TO
CHANGE THE HEART, MIND, AND SOUL
OF ALL THE LOST SOULS. CAUSE WE ARE
LIVIN' IN THE LAST DAYS. THERE ARE
NOT ENOUGH SAVED SOULS FOR JESUS'
RETURN, AND IT WILL BE SOON. SO LOST
SOULS, LISTEN TO THE GOOD STORIES
FOR OLD TIME'S SAKE, OR GET THROWN

IN THE BURNING LAKE, WHERE YOU CRY AND GRIT YOUR TEETH IN PAIN. WE SHOULD TEACH THE TRUTH ABOUT WHAT GOD WANTS HIS PEOPLE TO DO. FOLLOW IN JESUS FOOTSTEPS AND CONTINUE DOING HIS WORKS.

SPREAD THE LOVE AND BE A GREATEST GIVER

Remember That

It's over for you girl. I told you so. Before I let you go, can I get a kiss, hug and tap that back goodbye? I'm wrapping up, so I don't blossom your seed so you can come back to me. You want to leave me forever because my money is low. I was up before, and I'm goin' to do it again. This time it will last forever. Now you see me shining on TV. You want to come back into my life. Before you left me, I told you remember that. I tried to tell you I was going to shine one day, but you did not have faith in me. I found a Queen who stuck with me through my hard and low times. God blessed me with a whole new life. I can help my loved ones get out of debt and be on the same level as I am. No more suffering, worrying or pain. Our love for others on the right path is the same. With that power, we can win the battle over our enemies. We can live peaceful on Earth. My Queen loves me for me, not for my goals. Girl, you weren't right for me, but my Queen is. Now we are sitting on our thrones relaxing like a King and Queen by the glowing fireplace, drinking fine wine and listening to some soft music. Girl, you are missing all of this "his and her" this and "his and her" that. It could have been you if you had not turned your back on me. Just like God, I still love you. I guess you learned from your mistake. Now you're knocking at my door. I can't turn you away, so I'm asking you, "What can I help you with? Are you in debt? You need a car and a place to stay? You came to the right place for that. Only thing – I can't give you is me. Before I let you go, I just want to know ... are you on God's team? I would not want you to miss that flight (you know what I mean).

3 Throwin' Up Tres 3

Throwin' up tres, representin' my block. Everybody in my crew got at least four drops. Game in our cars can be heard at least three blocks. Ladies on the sidewalk screamin' out "Stop!"

Weavin' through traffic, lookin' in my mirror. Got a car full with ladies chasin' us down, so I slow down, roll down our windows to see what up. "Can we go with y'all?" " Not right now, but give me your name and number, and we can hook up later on." Typin' it in my two way. Turning off, screamin' out, "see y'all later on." Heading to the studio to finish my CD: *Job Well Done*. Sellin' 1,000,000 copies the first week I release it. All my business is done for today. Checkin' my two way to call up those ladies that we met earlier that morning. I'm going to have them come to the studio for a group session. It's about to go down. I have the video rollin'. The ladies ain't trippin'; partying all night long. Everybody passes out, except for me. I'm up, watchin' DVD's, playin' PS2, picking songs for CD number 2. I have a female eye-opener waiting for me to dig her before everybody wakes up, cause it will be time to go. It's a new day, business before pleasure. A daily routine: promoting my CD is better than chillin' with some high tech ladies – unless it's about some business (like want to feature her on a song with me). It's O.K. with me, cause I know we both are about our money. In just like the dope game. All money isn't good money, so watch who you deal with.

PLEASE BELIEVE IT

Please believe it, don't be surprised!
I worked hard for it so I'm going to floss it one life to live
so I'm living it
I'm rollin' a hummer H3 with 33's on my feet candy paint
5th wheel on the back leather guts ten 12 inch hearts
(speakers) beating super heavy duty veins (wires)

Connect to the brain (battery) so they can beat normal or
out of control
Yeah it's fat but it will never break a sweat
Keeping the coat clean my rims spin when I pause I can
drop my body to the ground like having a heart attack
Jump back up like nothing ever happened office theatre
and game room all in one the hole is wide open Everybody
can see me throwin' up tres representin' my block watch
and spinning rock on my pinky finger Flossing' I'm at home
playing eenie meenie miney mo with my toys

Picking' another one of a kind toy to jump in an 85 Chevy
van all brand new the top rolls back with a
Hole in the front candy paint 24s on my feet 5th wheel
on the back leather guts the back of the van is
Filled with speakers a big screen DVD with PS2 chrome

under body up and down the van goes while I roll The music is so loud you got to wear headphones while you roll I'm at a red light I need to stop but

My rims don't the law whips me for doing too much that's the devil just hatin' me and my family

Ain't nothing changed I still roll deep putting devils to sleep cause they always picked on me like a bully Those devils overlooked my powers they can't defeat me they see that now he's on God's side

They are too dirty to join His side if you're not clean or right He don't want you in His sight

He gave you a choice to turn left or right you turned left and ended up at a dead end

You could have turned right this is everlasting We could be side by side walking in the pearly gates are on a paradise earth but now it's too late.

PLEASE BELIEVE IT

CELEBRATIN'

celebratin' my first mill (million) plenty more to come business is picking up cause I'm not dumb spending money to make money keeping my mill on full watching my budget so I don't jack it off dressing so fly living so good rollin' so cold people want to know where I shop how many cribs I own what's the color year and cost of my whips (cars) I shop coast to coast and I can put a roof over everyone's head in my family the color is dry ice the year is 76 the cost is a little bit of nothing keeping my head up holdin' it down multiplying my business to make more money several different stash pots and they are all on lock down people see how good I'm living and want to go in on some of my business cause my name is making noise 24-7 worldwide who wouldn't want to ride on my team to make some money and have fun while they are still on earth if you have faith in god he will bless you the same I will celebrate that day every time it comes around rollin' a fat SS (Chevy Impala) just to catch a little buzz playtime is over stayin' busy is like a hobby to me can't be slippin' when it's time to collect my money coppin' again putting my profit up just like the dope game I'm in it to win it the law can't stop me in this game it will last longer than the dope game it's time to make a change throw the towel in it's over for the dope game your family and friends will be proud of you cause you will not be taking a chance getting caught by the law and being locked down like they want us to be or dead because they know when we work together the power we gain isn't too powerful and God will take out all the wicked people on earth

Mall Pimpin'

we enter the mall all eyes are on us ladies are walking up taking
pictures of us asking for hugs and autographs giving the number
to the ones that's good to go boys walking past looking and talking
some love us and some hate us but we have not a worry in the
world we know that they ain't going to step up to the plate and take
a swing so we head to the shoe store they love to see us cause
they know we are going to buy up the whole store pickin' out
shoes can I get these in all the colors we all paid a few hundred
dollars draggin' our bags before we walk out of the store they
say thank y'all have a nice day and see y'all next time now we
are heading to find fits to match each pair of shoes our hands
are already full but we are big boys we can handle it by now the
security is watching us go all the way to our cars loading up the
back seat with our bags cause the trunk is full with speakers and
amps after sellin' a few CDs everybody is ready to form a line
like a train rollin out jumping back on the highway headed back to
the hood parking on 32nd and Central to see what's the outcome
let's go to the studio everybody was like

let's go!

Comin' Up

Comin' up in the studio not out on the block sellin' work don't get me wrong I used to wake up get fresh and hit that word-33rd nickels and dimes of green 5-10-20 packs sting like killer bees stuffin' my pockets like a bag of leaves now you got to hit me on my two way for that book/CD look for me in your hometown store for **Street Stories/God's Glory Spread the Good News** spread the good news is blowing up like volcano so hot that we can't be stopped I'm going to hit your hometown roll around pick up a different hood girl would you like to ride on my BCR (big chrome rims) top down with surround sound playing with the switches headed to the room to join the party

comin' up

everybody is sippin' fine wine smoking good enjoying the girls from this hood Game and muscle is all we need for the hood girls to get busy but we don't want them to leave empty handed so we throw it up and it comes down like confetti got the girls smiling and feelin' good sayin' this is the best party I've been to since comin' up in the hood boys from here ain't doin' it like this? No! will ya'll be back? if the Lord's willing we are trying to make a change so if we make it back it won't go down the same "that's what's up!" We are going to try to do the same "Love and Peace" "Peace and Love"

Sittin' High and Well Respected

We both are sitting high seeing eye to eye
We are rolling up Illinois weaving and blowing
our horn like we just got married
Having fun well respected by them ones
They do have better things to patrol like other
ones
Trying to do what we do but get messed with
When the ones see us they let us do what we
do
Well respected like that knowing that the ones
have our back
Enough talk about that
If I'm goin' to brag on anything it wouldn't be
that
I will brag about the Lord to show His love
and to spread His love
Get into the Word and you will brag too
You will spread the good news It's all God's
plan for His people to do
Next thing you know you will be lookin' down
on the wicked ones
Seeing them on the chain line to watch them
burn
We make eye contact (that means to see eye to

eye) you will gain respect like that
Will you trust someone who can't' look you in
the eye
No
They won't survive unless they attack you from
the back
Only God knows where their hearts are
They are not sitting high and seeing eye to
eye
That's the wrong way to die, not sitting high
and seeing eye to eye with God

Parkin' Lot Pimpin'

In the club smellin' good dressed so fly
VIP's jumpin'
Ladies are coming wanting to join the
party
So they let us have it our way
To be chosen by some good guys from
Indianapolis
Pickin' only the ones that's good to go
By what they see they know what we are
whippin'
It's not hard cause we are VIP's
Every club we hit we get front row seats
Candy toys on 24's nothing little cause we
know that some ladies are leaving or
Following us that night switching whips
every other night
Candy toys on 22's for a personal night
Tour bus for a group session swerving but
I'm not perved
Some say I'm, crazy but I'm havin fun
Never leave home without packing my
video and Polaroid cause it's about to go
down Parking lot pimpin' after every show

We all packin big things so enemies don't
try us
Cause you will get tagged like we are
playing freeze tag
Puttin' and L on your fore head for loser
Callin' the law to come and pick you up
Callin' your Mom to make funeral
arrangements
She knows for a fact that we don't bother
nobody
That what he get but it hurts to lose a
loved one
She can't hold back her tears
We continue to enjoy our night of partying
at the hotel with the ladies

Cold and Deep, Hard and Nasty

My beats are cold my rhymes are deep   my music beats hard and
My nasty toy   (that's how I represent when I hit the streets)
My cold beats are produced at S S P studio   By my big cousin and Friends
My deep rhymes come from my heart mind and soul
                    I play my hard music around town
And my nasty toys   (that's how I represent when I hit the streets)
People respect my cold beats my deep rhymes
                    They hear my hard music beating and
See my nasty toy coming
                    (that's how I represent when I hit the streets)
People ask me where I get my cold beats from   My big cousin and Friends
Who writes your deep rhymes
ME!   Who plays your hard music.
Everybody in their home town
in Their nasty toys   (that's how I represent when I hit the streets)

Ladies like my cold beats like to hear my deep
rhymes
                              After a hard show
Get nasty with me
                              (that's how I represent when
I hit the streets)
 Haters down my cold beats and my deep rhymes
                                 But want my hard
          beating music
And my nasty toys   (that's how I represent
          when I hit the streets)

Workin' on the 8

I started with 2 jumped to 4
4 to 6 now I'm workin' on the 8
I'm living cool with my loved ones having faith
in God and me to complete my goals
Planning ideas to help the community giving
back because they gave to me
Getting stronger from the people who love and
respect me
I was hood rich supporting me and my loved
ones   I made it out of the hood
More people I can help to shine with me
"Ones who live by the truth will come to the
Light, because they want others to know that
God is really the One doing what thy do"
(John 3:21)
How evil ones from the darkside love that
They can't stand me because I'm sitting on
swole

Hitting hoods up in my candy drop top 6-4 or
my big body plus size (L-Dog) Town Car.
Pickin' up ladies that good to go don't mind
Dancing rub downs and posin' for Jiggy
Yeah, that's all I want to do
I can get that from my girl
Give me your number and I will give it to my
closest friend He will dig you and give you
M.D. just not me   Some say I'm crazy but
I'm just having fun   Don't be surprised I
just love to collect dancers.

God's Glory
The Second Half

Come and Take a Flight with God

Come and take a flight with God
on His wings
To a cloud far away
To be at peace.
Come in the shadow of God's wings and sing
happy songs.
He will help you stay close to Him. His
powerful arms will support you. Love each other
and all nations will be peaceful. All who desire
to kill you will end up in the ground chained
down with the devil.
God's people will celebrate in heaven while
singing praises to Him.
Dressed in a bright white robe with a crown on
our head and His name written on our foreheads.
The Lord God has many rooms in His mansion
for all of His people who obey and have faith.
The streets are made of gold. In front of His

throne is a crystal clear river that gives life.
Each one of us is a part of the body of Christ.
We were chosen to live together in peace with
thankful hearts. Sing psalms, hymns and
spiritual songs to God.

Come and Take a Flight with God!

SLIDE THROUGH

I'M CALLIN' MY FRIEND TO REFRESH MY MEMORY
IF I'M NOT MISTAKEN I'M SUPPOSED TO SLIDE
THROUGH DRESSED IN FINE WHITE LINEN
IT'S A PARTY TODAY AND IF I DON'T MAKE IT I
WILL LET MY PEOPLE DOWN
EVERYBODY IS HOPING TO GET OUR WINGS AND A
CROWN (JEREMIAH 8:7)
WE CAN STAY ALL DAY REST WHERE WE PLEASE
AND WAKE UP
KNOWING THAT WE ARE KINGS AND QUEENS
IT MUST BE NICE TO WEAR JEWELS
BETTER AND GREATER THAN DIAMONDS AND TO
SPREAD OUR WINGS AND GO ANY PLACE
BE ABLE TO COME AND LOOK DOWN AND HELP ALL
MANKIND SO THEY CAN JOIN THE PARTY AND
GET THEIR CROWNS AND WINGS AND TO REPEAT
THE SAME CYCLE FOREVER AND EVER
BUT SOME OF MANKIND WILL TURN OUR HELP
DOWN
THEY THINK THEY CAN SLIDE THROUGH
DRESSED IN FINE BLACK LINEN AND COME AND
GET IN THE PARTY

THEY DON'T MAKE IT AND THEY LET THEIR
PEOPLE DOWN
THEY WON'T BE GETTING WINGS OR A CROWN
CAN'T STAY ALL DAY AND REST WHERE THEY
PLEASE.
THEY WAKE UP KNOWING THAT THEY ARE NOT
KINGS AND QUEENS   IT MUST FEEL BAD
CAN'T WEAR JEWELS BETTER AND GREATER
THAN DIAMONDS
CAN'T SPREAD WINGS TO GO PLACES BUT ABLE
TO COME AND LOOK FOR A FEW OF MANKIND
TO JOIN THEIR PARTY AND GET NO CROWN OR
WINGS THEY REPEAT THIS SAME CYCLE JUST FOR
A SHORT PERIOD OF TIME (REVELATION 12:12)

ONLY 2 WAYZ TO GO

WE ALL START AT THE STARTING LINE OF BIRTH.
WE SHOULD GROW OLD AND RUN STRONG IN THE
RACE BUT SOME PEOPLE LIKE TO RUN IN THE DARK.
THEY KNOW ABOUT THE LIGHT BUT CAN'T FACE IT
DON'T LOVE IT.
THOSE PEOPLE IN THE DARK LIKE TO HELP THE
DEVIL THEY MIGHT RUN STRONG AND LONG BUT
AFTER DEATH THEY WON'T LIVE ON LIKE THE
PEOPLE IN THE LIGHT AFTER DEATH.
THE LIGHT WILL BE ON. THEY WILL SING AND PRAISE
GOD. GOD LOVES US ALL!
WHICH RACE WILL YOU RUN?
LIFE IS ROCKY, BUT DON'T GIVE UP!
GOD GIVES US A FREE WILL FOR A PURPOSE,
SO WE MIGHT HEAR, 'COME, YOU WHO HAVE BEEN
BLESSED BY MY FATHER, (MATTHEW 25:34) OR
"BE ON YOUR WAY FROM ME." (MATTHEW 25:41)
 FROM HIM AT THE FINISH LINE.

I'M ON FIRE

I'M ON FIRE RIGHT NOW   YOU CAN'T TAKE THIS
HIT.   YOU WILL SEE MY POWER.
I'M ON FIRE FOR THE LORD RIGHT NOW. YOU
CAN'T TAKE THIS NEW HIT BECAUSE IT IS
DIFFERENT
"HE WHO HATES ME HATES MY FATHER AS WELL"
(JOHN 15:23) YOU WILL SEE MY POWERS BY THE
MOVES I MAKE. I'M ON/UP HIGH. THE DARKSIDE
CAN'T TAKE THE HIT TRYING TO CUT OFF MY
POWER, BUT I'M WELL PROTECTED. GOD'S LOVE
IS ALL AROUND ME   I'M GLAD HE CHOSE ME TO
WRITE THESE ENCOURAGING LETTERS/ STORIES
TO ENCOURAGE A LOT OF PEOPLE. I AM SENDING
HIM TO YOU FOR THE EXPRESS PURPOSE THAT
YOU MAY KNOW ABOUT OUR CIRCUMSTANCES
AND THAT HE MAY ENCOURAGE YOUR HEARTS.
(COLOSSIANS 4:8)

THIS IS JUST WHAT THE WORLD NEEDS MORE
PEOPLE ON GOD'S SIDE/TEAM. THE DEVIL
IS MISLEADING THE WHOLE WORLD THUS
JEHOVAH REVEALED THAT IT IS HIS PURPOSE
TO EMPOWER A SEED TO CRUSH SATAN AND HIS

FORCES AND TO PROVE THE RIGHTFULNESS OF
HIS SOVEREIGNTY (PSALMS 110:1-2)
IT IS TIME TO SLOW DOWN STOP AND LISTEN
TO THESE HITS. JESUS TOLD ME "I AM SENDING
YOU TO THEM TO OPEN THEIR EYES AND TURN
THEM FROM DARKNESS TO LIGHT, AND FROM
THE POWER OF SATAN TO THE ALL MIGHTY
POWER OF GOD, SO THAT THEY MAY RECEIVE
FORGIVENESS OF SINS AND A PLACE AMONG
THOSE WHO ARE SANCTIFIED BY FAITH IN ME
(ACTS26:17-18) SO ARE YOU PAYING ATTENTION
TO ME?
I HOPE SO.
I'M ON FIRE!

ALL BRAND NEW

I'M GOING TO PRESS THE ISSUE OF CLEANING
UP THE COMMUNITY.
THIS IS WHAT I SEE THROUGH MY EYES:
EVERYTHING IS ALL BRAND NEW
EVERYBODY IS DOING GOOD AIN'T
THINKING ABOUT WICKEDNESS
I'M GOING TO START WHERE I LAY MY
HEAD AND THEN I WILL SPREAD THE ALL
BRAND NEW TOUCH
GETTING EVERYTHING FRESH AND CLEAN
BEFORE GOD COMES BACK.
YOU KNOW OUR FATHER WANTS THAT
(REVELATION 21:5)
HE'S USING HIS PEOPLE TO GET HIS WILL
DONE SO ALL MANKIND WAKE UP REPENT
AND
TURN FROM YOUR WICKED WAYS! ONCE
YOU DO YOU WILL BE DOING GOOD.
YOU WON'T THINK ABOUT WICKEDNESS BE
A PEACEMAKER AND JOIN WITH THE REST
OF GOD'S PEOPLE. THEN SPREAD THE ALL
BRAND NEW TOUCH BY HELPING OTHER
PEOPLE TO TURN FROM THEIR WICKED

WAYS, THAT'S GOD'S PROMISE/WILL. THEN
PRESS THE ISSUE OF CLEANING UP YOUR
COMMUNITY
BUT START WHERE YOU LAY YOUR HEAD
WHEN THE MAJESTIC JEHOVAH COMES
BACK
HE WILL RAISE HIS HAND AND SWEEP ALL
NATIONS FRESH AND CLEAN (1 SAMUEL 4:8)
A.B.N.
AMEN

STOP STALLIN'

LET ME STOP STALLIN' AND SPEED UP MAKIN' MOVES PAYIN' MY DUES AND MY FAMILY'S DUES NOW EVERYBODY IS PROUD OF ME. THEY MISS ME WHEN I LEAVE: THEY KNOW THAT I'M ALL ABOUT MY NET PAY THEY SAW ME COME UP BY STAYING IN TOUCH THEY KNEW THAT I WAS IN THE GAME, LET MY FAITH HANG THEY WORRY ABOUT ME GETTING HIT NOW I'M OUT OF THE GAME IT'S TIME TO SPREAD THESE STREET STORIES/GOD'S GLORY PROMOTING MY BOOK AND CD EVERYDAY OF THE WEEK LIKE BACK WHEN I WAS SELLING D (DOPE) UNTIL THE LAWS CAUGHT UP WITH ME NOW I'M SITTING IN THE PENITENTIARY WHEN I GET OUT I WILL GAIN CLOUT AN SHOW MY COMMUNITY WHAT I'M ALL ABOUT THEY KNOW I'M A TRUE

LIVING WITNESS OF A SAVED SOUL NOW WE ARE WORKING TOGETHER TO SPREAD THE GOOD NEWS TO ALL LOST SOULS IT'S JUST A MATTER OF TIME GOD'S PLAN WILL COME TOGETHER HE IS PUTTING ALL OF THE PIECES TOGETHER LIKE A PUZZLE HE IS THE ONLY ONE WHO CAN FIX IT ANYBODY ELSE WILL MESS IT UP CAN'T FIGURE IT OUT? GOD IS HERE TO COMPLETE IT IF YOU STAY CLOSE TO THE SON, YOU WILL HEAR A LOUD VOICE SAYING "JOB WELL DONE" LOOKING DOWN AT SOME PIECES THAT DIDN'T FIT AND I CAN'T WORRY ABOUT IT BECAUSE I'M AT A PLACE WHERE I CAN'T WORRY ANY MORE I ENJOY WORSHIPPING GOD WITH EVERY NATION TRIBE LANGUAGE AND PEOPLE SO STOP STALLIN' AND PICK UP THE CROSS TURN EVERYTHING OVER TO GOD SO HE CAN USE YOU TO SPREAD THE GOOD NEWS BOLDLY ENCOURAGE A LOT OF PEOPLE TO BE A GOOD PIECE, NOT A BAD PIECE OF THE PUZZLE YOU CAN CHOOSE THE WRONG BEND THAT'S WHY YOU DON'T FIT IN EVERY NATION TRIBE LANGUAGE AND PEOPLE CHOSE THE RIGHT BEND SO WE CAN SAY AMEN! PRAISE AND GLORY AND

WISDOM AND THANKS AND HONOR AND POWER AND STRENGTH BE TO OUR GOD FOREVER AND EVER AMEN!   (REVELATION 7:12)

STOP STALLIN'

My Peers

This is for my family peers that fell off the family tree. I'm lying in my bed at night thinking when it's goin to be me. To my family and friends I'm still lying in bed when another thought comes to my head: will I see my family and peers again? I hope that the good things they did outweigh the bad things they did. We all accepted the Lord into our hearts and were baptized. I pray before I close my eyes to rest. I wake up thanking God for seeing another day.

I'm getting fresh, doin' what I do best. Listening to what the rest of my family peers say. Nothing but good stories. I take them in just like reading the Bible. We were taught to get right before Jehovah God calls us home. We should all have a good score.

My Peers

I Got It

I got it now

My 1st half has come to an end

Let my 2nd half begin

You have to pay attention to your life cycle to know
that you controlled your 1st half and made mistakes

But God held onto you because He knew He could
use you in your 2nd half to reach a lot of people

Your 2nd half will be ten times greater

You will make less mistakes because

you learned from your 1st mistakes and

learned from other people's mistakes

So your 2nd time around should be great if you
let God control it

God does not make mistakes.

Amen!

Dark vs. Light

By listening to their head coach the devil the dark team thinks they can win.

The light team is rushing like football and messing up.

Now it's halftime: time to slow down stop and listen to God the head coach

Here's the plan: Y'all need to work together to get the job done.

The dark team is winning by a few points but I promise you by working together y'all will have victory over them

(1 Samuel 30:1)

It's time to start the 2nd half : everybody on three shout

"Victory 1-2-3 Victory!"

Everybody is going by the game plan, and at the end of the game the light team was the last ones standing with their hands in the air praising God, their head coach.

Amen!

Get Right

I'm a Star but I'm down to earth.

You can reach out and touch me and not get burned.

You can look at me and don't go blind.

Don't step to me the wrong way cause I can heat up and burn you and blind you all at the same time.

Do not touch my anointed ones; do my prophets no harm (1 Chronicles 16:22)

What happened to the peace and love?

Those days will come back around so don't give up.

Get your heart mind and soul right by praying to the

Lord to come into your heart.

Go to a church.

Repent and be baptized into the name of

the Father Son and Holy Spirit.

When you come up out of the water get
right.

Let the old man pass away and let the new
man live.
(11 Corinthians 5:17)

Ask God to order your steps so your days
will be filled with peace and love like the
days in the beginning of time. Amen.

Get Right

This is Deep - Part Two

The world is dyin' so I asked God to give me the power to heal it with my hands and words

I will slowly heal the world and

give God the glory (John 17:1)

Winning lost souls is my mission I was told by

God's will it will be done

Don't do what you tell others not to do because you are contradicting yourself

Go all the way straight

You won't lose the lost

More and more lost souls are being saved

The world can heal faster by us
working together

Unity is power that means all mankind

Diverse Unity

I thank God for everything

You should too because He's the one
who is doing it for you through you

Spread the word and you will see the
healing world

Earth will be like it is in Heaven
(John 17:4)

Wake up hear and see the truth

Don't be afraid the change is coming

Al le luia!

What's the Best Education You Can Get?

Knowledge Understanding and
Wisdom!

I worked my way up to the 10TH grade

Two more grades to go

My patience ran low but little
children keep on goin' don't give up

You and I should never stop learnin'

Because I didn't my peers taught me
the Bible words

A greater education the important one
of all

Complete this education all the way to
the end

The reward is everlasting

Finishing school is a nice reward but

IT CAN END THERE

TIMES ARE GETTING CRITICAL FOR
EVERYBODY

IT IS GOOD TO HAVE BOTH EDUCATIONS
BECAUSE BOTH WILL LAST TO THE END

THE KNOWLEDGE UNDERSTANDING AND
WISDOM YOU CAN GET FROM THE BIBLE IS A
HIGHER POWER

IT WON'T COME TO AN END

OUR HEAVENLY FATHER WILL HAVE A JOB/
POINT FOR YOU

NO MORE CRITICAL TIMES FOR ALL MANKIND

IT'S GOOD TO HAVE THIS KNOWLEDGE
UNDERSTANDING AND WISDOM BECAUSE IT

WILL LAST TO THE END.

AMEN.

Dig Down Deep and Finish Strong

I got off to a slow start in the word but I didn't give up. I dug down deep in the word and God's Holy Spirit transformed me from darkness to a marvelous light. I share it with all of those who will listen to me so we can finish strong in the race. So dig down deep and finish strong like training for combat, the days are hard but put your mind to it and you can do it (faith). Know your purpose here on earth is to train your heart and mind to become a Master worker (disciple).

Bring in the harvest (Matthew 9: 37-38) and complete the race with a good score so you can stand on that cloud with your hands in the air for victory over Satan the devil. Mission accomplished, job well done, you dug down deep and finished strong my people (Matthew 25: 31-46). It will be the world's greatest family reunion, we will have the last laugh and the devil and his angels (workers) will have the last cry. (Psalms 2:4, Psalms 126: 2). Your enemies will be your footstool (Psalms 110:1).

GET THE 1ST DOWN

WILL IT BE 4TH AND OUT OR WILL I GET THE 1ST DOWN? I KNOW MY BEST FRIEND/ FAITH WON'T LET ME DOWN. RECEIVE MY BEST FRIEND AND YOU WILL WIN THE RACE THAT IS SET BEFORE US (HEBREWS 12:1) THAT'S HOW YOU GET THE 1ST DOWN. RECEIVE MY BEST FRIEND, HE WON'T LET YOU DOWN, HE WILL PREPARE A PLACE (HOLY/ SOLID GROUND) FOR YOU (JOHN 14:2). SOUNDS GOOD TO ME, LET ME WORK ON GAINING/GETTING THE 1ST DOWN. YOUR BEST FRIEND INFLUENCES ME, HE'S LETTING US GET A VIEW OF HAVING EVERYTHING ON EARTH (ISAIAH 48: 17, 18).

THIS IS JUST THE RUFF DRAFT WAIT TILL YOU SEE THE FINAL COPY ITS AMAZING! EVERYTHING IS BRIGHT AND CLEAR LIKE MY BEST FRIEND AND MY BROTHERS AND SISTERS IN CHRIST. JESUS SAID: "YOU ARE MY FRIENDS IF YOU DO WHAT I AM COMMANDING YOU." (JOHN 15:14)... AND YET HIS COMMANDMENTS ARE NOT BURDENSOME, BECAUSE EVERYTHING THAT HAS BEEN BORN FROM GOD CONQUERS THE

WORLD. AND THIS IS THE CONQUEST THAT HAS CONQUERED THE WORLD, OUR FAITH (I JOHN 5:3, 4 AND I PETER 2:21).

IT'S 4TH QUARTER, 4TH AND INCHES AND ITS ALL ON YOU, THE GAME CLOCK IS WINDING DOWN. I HOPE YOU PICK THE RIGHT PLAY AND RECEIVE THE 1ST DOWN, BUT THE DEVIL IS BUSY. HE WALKS ABOUT LIKE A ROARING LION SEEKING TO DEVOUR SOMEONE... (I PETER 5:8). "KNOWING HE HAS A SHORT PERIOD OF TIME." (REVELATION 12:12). SO DON'T FUMBLE/STUMBLE CAUSE YOU MIGHT NOT GET ANOTHER PLAY (JEREMIAH 20:11). THE GAME OF LIFE CLOCK WILL SOON BE OVER, SO GET THE 1ST DOWN SO YOU CAN MOVE ON TO THE NEXT LIFE. (II PETER 3:9).

GET HIGH

I'M SO HIGH RIGHT NOW I DON'T WANT TO COME DOWN CAUSE ITS NATURAL. I CALL IT SPIRIT DOE (LOVE) IF YOU WANT SOME YOU CAN GET SOME BY STUDYING THE WORD, MAKE THE MEETINGS AND HANG WITH CHRISTIANS. TAKE 3 OF THESE AND CALL ME IN THE MORNING. WAS IT LOVE BUD? BRO THAT WAS LOVE (ACTS 26:28). I'M HOOKED ON IT AIN'T NOTHING WRONG WITH IT. I'M GLAD TO HEAR IT AND IT'S ALL FREE BRO THANK YOU FOR GIVING ME IT BRO I JUST LIKE TO SHARE BUT DON'T THANK ME THANK JEHOVAH. HE'S THE TOP CHIEF OF SHARING SPIRIT DOE (LOVE). I JUST GOT TO HAVE IT EVERYDAY AND I DON'T MIND SHARING IT.

SHARING LOVE LIKE THAT WHO CAN COMPLAIN, YOU WOULD BE SURPRISED. SOME PEOPLE CAN'T TAKE IT. I HEARD IT MAKES THEM FOLD UP (JOHN 10:13-18), THEY DON'T LIKE TO BE OPENED UP TO THE TRUTH, THEY WON'T SHARE THE

LOVE BUD, THEY JUST THROW IT AWAY
THEY WILL LIE AND SAY IT'S NO GOOD BUT
YOU KNOW THE TRUTH. SO PUT IN WORK
BY SHARING THE LOVE BUD ITS NOTHING
WRONG WITH IT IT'S GOOD FOR YOUR
HEART, MIND AND SOUL. SO KEEP IT IN
GOOD REPUTATION BY SHARING IT WITH
ALL MANKIND (I CORINTHIANS 12:13).

GET HIGH

Look Out/Be Honest

Keep your thermostat on 65 cool in the summer and your heat on 75 in the winter and you will be cool. Can't pay the bill don't worry they have programs for that, you have to network/ research for the help. It's not going to come to you, so go out there and find help. If you need it be honest, don't lie, it will mess you up on getting help. You might get away with it down here but not up there, don't let the devil trick you on thinking that, that's the way to get by, he's the father of the lie (John 8:44). He don't want to be the only one that be ruined at the end. (Romans 16:20).

I am pursuing down toward the goal for the prize of the upward call of God by means of Christ Jesus. (Philippians 3:14) (II Chronicles 16:9)

LIVE

To live you got/need to have blood, spirit and money (Romans 8:5-8).
Having the blood and the Spirit you will live after death. Having money you will live on earth.

Blood: Jesus said to him, "I am the way and the truth and the life..." (John 14: 6-8).

Spirit: Draw close to God and he will draw close to you. (James 4:8).

Money: Keep on, then, seeking first the kingdom and his righteousness and all these other things will be added to you.(Matthew 6:33)

Share these three with all mankind.

LIVE